THOUGHTS CREATE

Create Your Life from the Canvas of
Your Imagination

By:
DR. KAREN HYPOLITE

 TRILOGY

Trilogy Christian Publishers
A Wholly Owned Subsidiary of Trinity Broadcasting Network
2442 Michelle Drive
Tustin, CA 92780

For information, address Trilogy Christian Publishing
Rights Department, 2442 Michelle Drive, Tustin, Ca 92780.
Trilogy Christian Publishing/ TBN and colophon are trademarks
of Trinity Broadcasting Network.
For information about special discounts for bulk purchases,
please contact Trilogy Christian Publishing.
Manufactured in the United States of America

10 9 8 7 6 5 4 3 2 1
Library of Congress Cataloging-in-Publication Data is available.
ISBN 978-1-63769-148-9
ISBN 978-1-63769-149-6 (ebook)

TO TORI

TABLE OF CONTENTS

PREFACE

This is not just a regular book. This is a power tool to add to your toolbox on your way to living the life of your dreams; a life of purpose and destiny. Prepare to be inspired, motivated, and encouraged.

It is divided into 3 parts:

1. Understanding How Thoughts are Things

2. Dealing with old negative thought patterns (out with the old and in with the new)

3. Using your new thoughts to actually create the life of your dreams

You will be armed with tools, tips, and strategies to use your mindset as an asset to create your life. With God's Word as the guidepost, you'll learn how to use your thoughts for you and not against you. Also, learn how to use thinking as an actionable force to create your life. Always remember, the life of your dreams is waiting... for YOU to create it.

xoxo,

Dr. Karen

INTRODUCTION

Thoughts are things. They are not just random or haphazard bits of information that roll around in our heads. Thoughts create! They have a physical counterpart. They regulate circumstances, situations, and atmospheres. They have the power to attract and repel, including attracting people to us or repelling people away from us! Our thoughts create our reality. They dictate our very lives.

Thinking is an actionable force. It is a creative agent of life. Thoughts create.

We have the power to control, manage, and direct our thoughts. You have the power to direct your thoughts at will. Your life doesn't have to happen to you. You can happen to your life. By thinking the right thoughts, you create the atmosphere around you. The right atmosphere around you will attract all the good you desire to come to you, thus creating the life of your dreams. You can have the life you were destined to live:

9

a life of victory, power, and authority. Living the life of your dreams is possible. Yes, the life you want is waiting…for *you* to create it!

Thinking is an actionable and very powerful force. It is harnessed with scientific precision by very few for specific outcomes and results. We have the power to control our thoughts for a specific outcome. Whether intentional or just left random, thoughts create! For the sake of this book, we will not get into the technical details of the electrical firing in the brain that transmit thought. However, we will get into the procedural intentionality of thoughts and their results.

> Everything we do as humans begins with a thought. Thinking is as natural as breathing and it is a creative function of life.

Everything we do as humans begins with a thought. I did not realize how important my thoughts were. I did not realize that there was a life I was creating within my control—that was out of control. I did not realize that my thoughts had everything to do with my life being out of control. The life I had always wanted was not the life that I was living.

We have the power to control our thoughts with intentionality and specificity.

As I began to learn and to understand how to direct my thoughts with the Word of GOD, I had it within me the power to live my dreams: God's dream for me. For many years, I thought I was waiting on GOD, but He was waiting on me. The more I learned, the more I wanted to know about this power-packed life that God had in store for me using my thoughts.

Living My Dreams

Wouldn't it be wonderful to live the life of your dreams, a life full of victory and blessings everywhere you looked? It would be so beautiful if happiness and contentment was your normal state of being: your health flourishing, financial resources in abundance, with relationships harmonious. Living a life of purpose and meaning would actually be an everyday occurrence. It would be a life where your soul is filled with joy and peace, and you were free of bondage, sickness, disease, anger, frustration, and depression. Unfortunately, many people are not living the life of their dreams. In many cases, living the life of one's

> The life you want is waiting....
> for You to create it!

dreams can be the exception instead of the rule, but that's not how God designed our lives to be. For many, the struggle is real, and there always seems to be something left to be desired. Either the successes of their life were few and far between, or they were not in every area of their life. This can change. There is good news. There is a way through. I found it in

God's Word. The life you want is waiting for you to create it, and I'll show you how!

Foundational Scriptures

"Let this mind be in you which was also in Christ Jesus." (Philippians 2:5).

"Be not conformed to this world, but be ye transformed by the renewing of your mind that you may prove what is that good and acceptable and perfect will of God." (Romans 12:1-2).

PART 1

Thoughts Are Things

Chapter 1

THE BACK STORY

How It All Started

Genesis 1:1 gives us a snapshot of the original creative process. God is the Creator, Originator, and Progenitor of *all* things: living and non-living. God the FATHER, God the Son, and God the Holy Spirit were all present in the beginning. Every part of the creative process originated in the mind of God. Thought is the origin of that which is to be created. God the FATHER is the source of the thought of what He wanted to create before He spoke all of life into existence. The Spirit of God was present, brooding over the water right before He spoke. Jesus, the Son of God, was there in Word form. How do we know? Because John 1:1, 3 says "In the beginning was the Word, and the Word was with God, and the Word was God...All things were made by him; and without him was not any thing made that was made."

> Genesis 1:26 And GOD said, "Let us make man in our image, after our likeness: and let them have dominion.."

GOD has thoughts. GOD thinks and

speaks His thoughts.

Scripture tells us that God has thoughts. Psalms 92:5 says, "O LORD, how great are thy works! And thy thoughts are very deep." Also Jeremiah 29:11 says, "I know the thoughts that I think towards you, saith the LORD." So, it's safe to say that God's thoughts proceed out of His mouth. He used His voice, spoke, and the "worlds were framed by the word of God, so that the things which where are seen were not made of things which do appear" Hebrews 11:3. We have been endowed with the exact same ability. We have it within us to create our world the same way God did His (see Genesis 1:26). You and I are responsible for creating our life using the same means and parameters that have

As humans, we are naturally creative beings. Primary of our creative ability comes from thinking, just like GOD does.

been bestowed upon us, and it all begins with our thoughts. Now that we have an understanding of the framework God used to create the world and everything in it, we are armed with the right tools to begin the process of our thoughts creating our lives. One thing to note, Satan is our enemy. The enemy's #1 warfare tactic against believers is in the mind: evil thoughts and imaginations to interrupt our creative ability. We will discuss in further detail later in this book the rules of engagement to defeat every negative thought.

Created with God-Abilities

God created us in His image and likeness (see Genesis 1:26). Likeness is a special term. The Holy Spirit wanted to make it clear that we were created to be like God and to have God's abilities, creating being primary of them. As we gain an understanding of how thoughts create, we first must understand our make up as humans and how God created us to exist in the Earth. We are laying the groundwork, or grasping the rules of engagement, for how our thoughts function in us and in this world around us. This prepares us to create the life Jesus died for us to have.

The worlds and the humans that live therein are
governed by laws; the framework and infrastructure
for our existence.

Although we are spiritual beings created in the image and likeness of God, we are spirit-beings living in a physical body. Our existence is governed by laws which govern both the physical and spiritual worlds. We are governed by the laws that govern these two worlds simultaneously, which mirror each other. This is borne out of the fact that when Jesus prayed, he said, "Thy Kingdom come, Thy will be done on Earth as it is in Heaven" (see Matthew 6:10). We live in a world governed by physical laws as spirit-beings that govern our walking around every day lives. And because we are spirit-beings, we are subject to spiritual laws as well, even though we live in a human body on Earth. For example, on Earth we put seeds into the ground and the seeds bring forth fruit, trees, and grain. So, it is in the spiritual world, we are governed by laws of the spirit realm that govern spiritual principles. For instance, a spiritual principle is, "Be not deceived; God is not mocked for whatsoever a man soweth, that shall he also reap. For he that soweth to his flesh shall of the flesh reap corruption; but he that soweth to the Spirit shall reap life everlasting" (See Galatians 6:7-8). Jesus bore out the fact that actions on Earth had reactions in Heaven. We will discuss later in detail the privilege, responsibility, and the delegation of authority Jesus gave Peter to operate in the natural world and in the supernatural world.

> Heaven and Earth were designed to mirror each other.

Thoughts Reproduce After their Kind

Everything was meant to reproduce after its own kind. The seed is the thing in which it will produce. A man plants a seed into a woman and another of mankind is produced. Pumpkin seeds produce pumpkins. Apple seeds produce apples. Acorns produce oak trees. We can also reference thoughts the exact

18

same way. Thoughts are things! And they reproduce after their own kind. Negative thoughts meditated on consistently will produce negative results. Positive thoughts meditated on consistently will produce positive results.

Thoughts create 100% of the time.

Everything begins with a thought. As human beings, we were given the ability to create using our thoughts. This ability was bestowed upon us at creation in the Book of Genesis. We had this ability at birth. Thinking creatively is just as natural as breathing. We do it automatically, yet subconsciously. **Thoughts create 100% of the time.**^{SM} Our creative ability using our thoughts works 24 hours a day, seven days a week, 365 days a year, or 366 days on a leap year. This ability has been activated since the moment we were born and will continue. It doesn't shut off. It happens automatically and

> Thoughts have an intended consequence; positive or negative and good or evil.

at will without any additional help. Just like we were created with the ability to walk, talk, and eat, we were created with the ability to create with our thoughts. Just as our natural-born ability to walk, to talk, and to eat had to be cultivated for us to function properly with them, so it is with our ability to think and to create. We have to cultivate our power to create the life that we want with our thoughts the exact same way.

Power to Choose

Please understand that we can use our thoughts in a positive way or negative way. Our thoughts can work for us or against us. What I have come to understand, and have been able to put into practice, is that I have it within me to choose my thoughts. As an act of my will, I volitionally think thoughts that are congruent with the life that I desire to create. With the Word of God, I cast down every thought that is incongruent with the life I desire to create. The constant audit of thoughts and what to do with them is key!

As with any law, working in conjunction with them yields good results. Working against them yield bad results. Newton's Third Law of Motion states that for every action there is an equal and opposite reaction[1]. A tennis ball bouncing against the ground will return with equal and opposite force. So it is in the spirit world it is in the natural world. Proverbs 23:7, "As a man thinks in his heart so is he." There is 0^0 of separation between who you are and what you think. Proverbs 4:23 says, "Guard your heart with all diligence, for out of it flows the issues of life." One thing that must be clear is that there are specific rules that accompany the phenomena of creation. We will cover them in-depth in this book. At the end of this book, you will be able to, with exactness of precision, execute your thoughts like a scientific procedure borne out into mechanical practice.

CHAPTER QUESTIONS

1. Do you believe you have creative ability just like GOD?

2. What area(s) of your life could use your intentional thoughts to make any changes?

3. How would you change the way you think now?

Chapter 2

The Life You Want

———

The life you want, the happiness, the joy, the peace, the health, the relationships, the marriage, the children, the house, the finances, or anything else in this life that you desire, is waiting for you. **Life is inside out, not outside in.** Many of us have been waiting for years, myself included, for our lives to change. I can remember year after year saying, "Maybe this year things will change. Maybe this is the year things will get better." Every year that my mindset and my thoughts did not

> All actions of life begin with a thought. Life is inside out, not outside in.

change, things stayed the same. Why? I did not put the things in my thoughts that I wanted to see in my life. I did not apply the force of the Word of God to it. I let myself become subject to my surroundings. I refer to this as living trapped in the death cycle.

Normal isn't normal in The Death Cycle

Everything around us seems to be negative. There are things said and constantly repeated in our world and in our culture that seem normal. You've heard them just as I. Things such as, "Things will never change." "I never get any good breaks." "It will always be this way." The reason why things never change for people who keep this mentality is because they think things will never change. As the mentality, so is the life. I thought the same things. Yet it never dawned on me that I actually could do something about my life changing. It was within my control. The outcome of my life was within my purview. I actually had a say. I was not the subject or victim of anyone or anything. I actually had influence over the outcome of my life. I did not have to settle for someone else's version of what my life should be. I was not limited to other people's limitations or expectations of the life I called my own. I had something to do in preparation for the life that I had always wanted. Many times, I felt trapped—trapped in someone else's life. My dream world was screaming, "This is not it." My contemporaries, and even my family and friends, could not see the life I could see. It was my real life, the life I had always dreamed of living.

> The life of your dreams is as real as your present life. You must use your thoughts to turn your dreams into reality.

My Life... My Responsibility

I, like many people, was not taught how my thoughts work. I knew very little about the life axiom that our thoughts control our life. I was waiting for something or someone outside of me to change my life. I thought that something outside of me was responsible for how my life turned out. I thought life happened to me. I did not realize that I had the power to happen to my life, direct my life, and tell my life what to do. I had it within my power to direct the outcome and the results of what I produce, and my life was a reflection of it. I learned that life is what you make of it, and the origin of its creation begins with a thought.

For years, I was spinning my wheels: going nowhere fast. It was exhausting. I prayed, and nothing changed. Then, I finally wondered, *what could be the reason?*

Something was missing and I knew it.

Why was I not seeing the results of the life I wanted? Why wasn't anything changing? What was I missing? I had great ideas, great connections, great opportunities, but nothing took off. Why? It was my mindset. It was my own self-defeating and self-sabotaging thoughts that held me captive. There is a three-step process I went through that set me free. It took something bigger than me, but it also included me. Once this process occurred, I was free! My thoughts began to shape my life based on what I created. As my understanding of how this process worked progressed, I began to create the life I wanted, and it started happening like clockwork.

Big Misunderstanding

As absurd as it might seem, as a Christian, I thought that the mind's power to produce thought and mind control was of a secular nature. Somehow, I was under the impression that I was to focus on my spirit and people who focused on "mind power" were either agnostic or atheist. Whether people have no faith in anything beyond the physical or don't believe in GOD at all is immaterial. Upon creation, we were created and designed to live and function in this natural world. Living and breathing as a human being requires the use of the human faculties. The everyday walking-around life requires an act of the will, the imagination and, yes, thought. Yet, knowing what to do with our thoughts is a different story. These human faculties were given to us by design. A carpenter that has tools without the skills to use them is useless in the building process. However, tools in the hands of

> You do not have to settle for a humdrum sort of life. You can live the life GOD promised you.

a skilled master carpenter can build something beautiful that lasts a lifetime. I don't recall ever fully understanding how to employ these human faculties in tandem with the power of the Spirit of God to produce results in my life: the life I wanted and the "life more abundantly" that God had promised me.

Before, I was living, but it was a pseudo-life. It was as though the life of my dreams in my imagination was real and my everyday world was unreal. I knew there was so much more to life, because I was not okay with how things were. Something deep within me was calling for greater and calling for more. So, I started searching for more, and God led me to more. The more I learned, the more I gained freedom. Empowered with this new information, I was experiencing a level of peace, liberty, and security that I had not known before. I was no longer a victim of my circumstances, other people's opinion of me, or held captive as a prisoner to my own thoughts that I was undeserving and unworthy of the life of my dreams. Riddled with fear, doubt, unbelief, failure, defeat, inadequacy, insecurity, insufficiency, and oppression, I would sabotage every opportunity of growth and success that came my way. The results of these negative, toxic, and self-deprecating thoughts were lack, sickness, loneliness, failure, and the list goes on.

The more I understood the power of my thoughts and that I had the power to choose which thoughts I would keep and which I would rid myself of, the more I began to see results and to live a victorious life. It hit me! I can choose the thought. Therefore, I can choose the outcome! A positive thought with a positive outlook leads to a positive outcome. A negative thought with a negative outlook leads to a negative outcome, regardless of the circumstance. It was all beginning to make sense to me now.

Choose the thought, choose the outcome.

Thinking as a Scientific Procedure.....?

As a scientist, I found it to be no coincidence that the scientific laws and principles I studied for many years could be found mirrored in God's Word. It was then that I realized there was a connection between the physical world and the spiritual world. The more I studied, the more I realized that being intentional with my thoughts could be a scientific procedure borne out in mechanical practice. It would be a series of if-then actions to determine a specific outcome. If this thought comes, then do this... for every thought every time, "leading every thought captive to the obedience of Christ" (see 2 Corinthians 10:5).

Scripture says, "Faith comes by hearing, and hearing by the Word of God" (see Romans 10:17). It is also why Jesus said, "Be careful how you hear" (see Matthew 4:24). With this new information, the life I was born to live, life more abundantly (See John 10:10), was now within my reach. Some would say I focused on the major rather than the minor. Secularists would say I focused on the minor rather than the major. Well, which is which? Was I to put all my energy and focus into prayer and let my thoughts run wild? Was I to put all of my energy into focused concentration and intense philosophical thought without giving consideration to my spirit, the FATHER of all spirits from Whom my spirit came (See Hebrews 12:9), or the place where my spirit would dwell after this life? What I came to understand, I will share with you later in this book. As a

---

As a spirit-being living in a physical world, I must give attention to my spirit and my mind.

---

spirit-being living in a physical body living in a physical world, I must give attention to both. Not only was I to pray and ask GOD for grace, mercy, direction, and provision, but also I was to direct my thoughts to that end. Which end? I was to direct my thoughts to the end of which I had prayed. You see, what I learned is that GOD has a role, and I have role in this life. I gave attention to part of the spirit world, but neglected the natural world. Yet, I could not understand why I was not getting the results for that which I had prayed. I prayed and asked GOD one day why my life was a mess as a believer. In a still, small voice I was directed to my inner world. Not my spirit, where Christ lives, but my mind where "I" lived, so to speak.

In order for the power of God to work in my life, I had to let Him work. Whenever Jesus went to heal someone or to deliver them, he would always get their input, "Do you believe that I can do this or that." It was the same with me. He could not work beyond what was in me.

Because as much as He wanted me healed, healing could not supersede my unbelief if I thought healing was not for me. The same was the case of the people in the hometown of Jesus. Scripture tells us, "Now He could do no mighty work there, except that He laid His hands on a few sick people and healed them. And he marveled because of their unbelief. And he went round about the villages, teaching" (see Mark 6:5-6). Even GOD Himself was limited to what He could do in the lives of people because of their limited thinking. Conversely, the woman with the issue of blood had a different approach. "For she said within herself, 'If I may touch but his garment, I shall be whole'" (see Matthew 9:21). She thought differently and received a different result. She was healed. Her mindset was a determined one. The same thing happened for me. I made a decision. I was determined that my life could, should, and would be better. The better I thought it would be, the better my life became.

> In order for GOD's power to work in me, I had to let Him.

Chapter Questions

1. What negative cultural narratives seem reoccurring to you?

2. What Promises have GOD spoken over your life that seem impossible?

3. What limiting thoughts do you have that could prevent the promises of GOD from coming to pass in your life?

Chapter 3

POWER THOUGHTS: UNLEARN THE LEARNED

I know what you have learned. It's the same thing I learned. We have picked things up by osmosis, by listening to others. Some of these would include commonalities in popular culture, family stories, gossip, or someone else's experiences. Until recently, this was my paradigm. And like many of you who did not take considerable time to evaluate what you believe, what you think, and the realities of your life thereof, this became your paradigm.

The Paradigm

A paradigm is a mental program, a way of thinking, or menagerie of thoughts and ideas that somehow become your own. There is no solid organization of principles upon which to build your life. Some of us arbitrarily developed a paradigm—a way of thinking, a mentality, a frame of mind, a system of processing information, a consciousness without understanding the consequence of what we decided was true. Oftentimes, it's based on the closest, most readily available, or most prevalent information.

A Paradigm from The Ancient of Days - The Basis for My Thought

---

There is another way of developing a paradigm. The most powerful, effective, and results-driven paradigm way is what I have discovered. It just makes sense to pattern my thoughts after the One who created everything. The highest form of consciousness is the consciousness that is aligned with the laws that govern the spiritual and physical worlds—the laws of God. From where do they come? How did they start? Who started them? "In the beginning, GOD…" It took me a while to understand that my thoughts had consequences. Uninvited thoughts, bad thoughts, negative thoughts, evil thoughts, all came to my mind, and I did not do anything with them. I just waved them off, hoping they would go away. But remember, thoughts are things. Thoughts take up mental real estate and, unless you do something with them, they activate their physical counterpart. We do it unconsciously and, unless we are intentional about these little creative agents, thoughts unchecked will create. And what we don't want will show up in our life.

Thoughts are powerful

Thoughts have tremendous power! Our thoughts control our reality! Second to salvation through Jesus Christ, some of the greatest news of all time is that you have the power to choose which thoughts you think, which thoughts will control your life, and which thoughts will create your life. Thoughts are things! They can translate us from one state of being to another: from anger to happiness, from sadness to joy, from disappointment to excitement. Thoughts are very powerful! If we learn and understand how to harness the power of our thoughts, we stand to gain insight on how we have the power to change our very lives and to live life more abundantly.

Have you ever been thinking about something or someone, and then soon after you saw that very thing or person? You may have even said to them upon sight, "I was just thinking about you." Or you might have said, "I was just thinking about that." Have you ever been surprised that something you had been thinking about showed up? It's no coincidence. There is an actual science to something showing up in your life that you thought about. Thoughts in our inner world are connected to our outer world. I often ponder on the power that we have as human beings—a power innately given to us upon creation.

Life by Design

Like an architect sees a building in his mind before he puts it on paper, so it is

Creatives throughout history harnessed the power of their thoughts and changed the world.

with our thoughts. We have to see it in our mind's eye before we can see it in real-time. That is when the ownership transfer of what you see begins to take place. There can be challenges. Unexpected events may occur that could not have possibly been foreseen by the architect, and some things just cannot be avoided. But the architect does not throw in the towel and, halfway through the building project, throw up his hands and say, "Forget it." Or say something to the effect of, "It must not be for me to build this building." The same goes for the engineer who designs a car, or a machine, or robot. Where would we be today if creatives all over the world decided that what they created with their mind was not worth creating in real-time? Where would we be as the human race? Creatives advance human civilization. We have many examples of past creatives who harnessed the power of their thoughts and changed the course of their lives and history.

Thoughts create things that are both tangible and intangible. Some people's thoughts invented products, brands, or even opportunities. We have biblical, historical, and contemporary examples of both men and women who used their thoughts to create, overcome adversity, and live out their dreams. What

---

Creatives and thinkers transcend their current life to their Promised life.

---

about Noah? The Earth had not yet rained when he built the ark. The Shunammite woman with her dead son in her hand who professed all was well. Sarah's thoughts strengthened her to have a child past childbearing age. Madame C.J. Walker's thoughts, inspired by a dream, invented a product that made her the first female self-made millionaire in America, according to the Guinness Book of World Records[2]. Steve Jobs', along with Ronald Wayne's and Steve Wozniak's, thoughts created the Apple brand, revolutionizing how we process, communicate, and share information around the world. Fredrick Douglas' and Harriet Tubman's thoughts created pathways to freedom from slavery. Susan B. Anthony's thoughts created opportunities for the abolishment of slavery and for women's suffrage, as Dr. Martin Luther King, Jr.'s thoughts created the momentum for the Civil Rights Movement. Dr. Lonnie Johnson's thoughts revolutionized the toy water gun. Elon Musk's thoughts sought to revolutionize transportation here on Earth and in Space. I could go on and on with pages upon pages of people without notoriety who have accomplished great feats using their thoughts. Not without their challenges, the success of each of these creations, whether products, brands, or opportunities, began with a thought.

The life you want is waiting on you... to CREATE it! Left unchecked, the outer influences of society, There is a three-step process I have found for this transformation to take place.

37

pop culture, negativity, past mistakes, failures, or traumatic life experiences try to dictate the life that we live. I am here to share with you that through the wisdom and power of the Holy Spirit and practical steps I have incorporated into my life, I have been able to create the life that I desire. This book will outline the three factors that impact the understanding of how thoughts create, and they include: 1) How the thoughts we think work in real-time 2) Negative influences on thoughts 3) Everyday practical steps to the creative process through thought.

Thinking creatively is as much a privilege as it is a responsibility.

I want you to understand and to appreciate that, as a human being, we have been given a precious gift, a gift not given to any other species of animal on this planet. We can CREATE! This is what differentiates us from monkeys, elephants, and giraffes. We were created in the image and likeness of God ALMIGHTY. As a creation scientist, I would like to take a pause and point out that a species of lower intelligence does not have the capacity to produce a species of higher intelligence. Upon creation, we were endowed with dominion over every living creature on the planet. With this endowment came a privilege and a responsibility.

Our thoughts were the mechanism that God chose to activate actions and results for our life here on Earth as spirit-beings. Thoughts are things that take up mental real estate. They have power to create or to destroy. I want to share with you how to use your thoughts to create the life that you want. The life you want is waiting…for YOU to create it! There is a real methodology to how thoughts work in relation to how our life works. Thoughts used properly determine the outcome of your life's success. Thoughts used improperly determine your life's demise.

Take Away: We have the power to control our thoughts.

Living according to principles that govern the physical and spiritual worlds guarantees success. Why? It is due to the fact that laws give us rules of engagement. They provide a framework for which everything can work. And they provide security, norms, and an infrastructure from which we are to operate. If not, then we have total chaos, catastrophe, calamity, and human casualties. A good example of this would be the laws of the highway. The laws of the highway do not necessarily control us. They give us rules of engagement for everyone to remain safe and unharmed. This is exactly how we engage our thoughts.

CHAPTER QUESTIONS

1. Do your own thoughts intimidate you? Why?

2. What misconceptions or misunderstandings can you pinpoint that have caused an interruption in your creative thinking abilities?

3. Can you list or name anyone personally who has achieved such notable accomplishments by the way they think?

PART 2

Thoughts - The Dark Side

Chapter 4

THE INTERRUPTION: THE GOOD WITH THE BAD.

Here We Go

66We interrupt this regularly scheduled program..." is what you might have heard while listening to your favorite radio or television show. An unexpected interruption to what was planned had occurred. This is how our lives have been since the Garden of Eden—until Jesus. Do you want the good news or the bad news? Okay, bad news first...We are in a battle. Now the good news... Jesus Christ won it!!! And, although we face opposition, we have the tools necessary to overcome it all. The truth of the matter is you have the same creative ability as God: the MOST HIGH. He created you and me with the creative ability to create just like He created. PERIOD. You and I have the power within to create the life God put it in our hearts to live. God put that dream, that desire, that passion in you. So, why are you not living it? Because of two things: 1) lack of knowledge and 2) enemy interference. Once you have the information, you will know how to disrupt the interruption and do what you were created to do...CREATE. We have been given all the tools and the authority to win every encounter. That's why we have Jesus.

It's not the devil, people, or any other force. The word of the LORD says, "My people are destroyed for lack of knowledge." (see Hosea 4:6). We cannot walk out and live out something we don't know.

The Good Life

Walking with God in the cool of the day, a perfect marriage, a garden that watered itself, and a pot of gold was mankind's destiny. This was to be our lot in life. What changed it? It all started with the enemy that presented itself and the worst bite of fruit in human history. What became of it you might ask? The curse was activated: the descent of marriage, sickness, lack, physical labor and, worst of all, a choice between good and evil. Thus, sin and death fell on every man since.

JESUS CHRIST - The WAY back to Eden

God put Himself in a body named Jesus Christ. Jesus died to set us free, to be like Him in every way. Jesus obliterated the law of sin and death. All that was left was for us to find out how to use this freedom that Jesus paid for with His own body and blood. The rights for us to be in perfect union with God and perfect alignment with our God-like abilities was given away in the garden by Adam, but Jesus got them back for us. The entire ministry of Jesus' preaching was about the Kingdom of Heaven and the Kingdom of God. He came in human form to show us directly what we have the ability to do in human form with Him working on the inside of us. PERIOD. Well, there is someone who doesn't want this to happen. Why? It is because we as humans can do what he cannot. With a failed attempted coup of the throne of GOD in Heaven, losing his job, being kicked out of Heaven by God, condemned to eternal damnation at the appointed time and replaced by mortals, he is our true enemy. Subsequently, the enemy wanted what GOD gave to Adam—dominion.

Interference Causes Disruption

Why do we have bad thoughts? Why do negative thoughts come into our mind? From where do negative thoughts come? What is the origin of these thoughts of failure, fear, defeat, shame, hurt, pain, sorrow, death, etc.? Why do we have to deal with this evil that comes to interrupt our life flow? In life there is God. God has an enemy: the devil. God's enemy became our enemy. Our life became the constant battle of evil trying to outdo good, but it never works. Jesus took his power, so all he has is an antagonistic approach. He wants to bug you, distract you, accuse you, lie to you, and deceive you until you give up. Just like in life, or any sport for that matter, football in particular, you have two opposing sides. One is advancing the

> Victory is the only response when we are faced with attacks on our thoughts.

ball to score and to win. The other is doing everything they can to stop that from happening. It is the theme of every story ever penned by man, and it is part of life. And so the story goes, it is in the life of your thoughts.

Since thoughts create and you have an enemy, wouldn't it stand to reason that, to defeat you, he would send thoughts to your mind that did not originate with you for your demise. God's thoughts toward us are good. He said, "For I know the thoughts that I think toward you, saith the LORD, thoughts of peace, and not of evil, to give you an expected end" (see Jeremiah 29:11). So, that is our foundation. God wants good for you. Therefore, that is the expectation. That is the standard. You were created by God, and you were created for good. The opposition wants the exact opposite for your life. "The thief comes but to steal, kill, and to destroy. Jesus said, "I come that thou may have life and life more abundantly" (see John 10:10). There you have it: the story of our life. Abundant living through Jesus Christ is available to every man, woman, boy, and girl. So how do we get it? First, we've established that there is a connection between what thoughts you think and the life you live. Now, we delve into the current processes of your thoughts and how to change them. Change your thoughts! Change your life!

Chapter Questions

1. From where does the source of evil thoughts come?

2. Why do evil thoughts come?

3. What scripture tells us about the thoughts that GOD has toward us and how can we use them for our advantage?

Chapter 5

THE DIRTY WORK

There is no way for me to tell you the process of shifting the paradigm of my life from lies to the truth and of understanding my ability to create my life with my thoughts was easy. It actually was excruciatingly difficult. Since my life was in my thoughts, it was as if my entire life was shifting on its axis to an entirely new direction. The lift was heavy, but God's WORD did most of the work. I just used the act of my will to let it happen. I was a caterpillar fighting for my life to be free of a hardened, constricting outer shell of something

My Dad had a saying from the Marine Corps. "It's hard, but it's fair." The work to get to your destiny is worth it.

that I knew did not feel like me. It didn't look like me. Little did I know, the fight, the struggle, and the pain were what shaped me into who I am today. Like the caterpillar that transformed into a butterfly, today I am the best version of my current self on my way to my destiny. My life shifted from potentiality to actuality, and it feels marvelous. For what I know today, how

I feel today, and what my life is like today, it was all worth it. My freedom was worth it. My soul peace was worth it. For my sense of self-love, confidence, and security, it was all worth it.

Clean Up on Aisle Seven

I had several layers of lies working in my life that I allowed to hold me back. Some were imposed on me and others were self-imposed. Regardless of the source, I had to deal with them

----

Facing yourself is one of the hardest things you will ever do.

----

all. Knowing the truth sets us free (see John 8:32). Jesus is the Way, the Truth, and the Life (see John 14:6). And, "the truth is in Jesus" (see Ephesians 4:21). Exposing the lies of the enemy and replacing them with the truth of God's Word sets us free. The fact that our thoughts create and shape our lives is true. The fact that we have the power to cast down every lying thought and imagination and to make it obey Christ is true (see 2 Corinthians 10:4-5). This is how the work begins: 1) Accept God's Word as final authority 2) Follow the tools and strategies it provides for complete success. When applied properly, the Word of God has a 100% success rate.

By now, we understand that, by nature, thoughts create. God is very precise. In His Omniscience, He established our world and our existence in it so that the laws that govern the physical

> When applied properly, the Word of God has a 100% success rate.

and spiritual worlds work in conjunction with our thoughts. That is how the system is set up. The thoughts we think, good or bad, have a direct impact on what shows up in our lives. If thoughts can create, then thoughts can destroy. Thoughts can build us up or they can keep us held captive—a prisoner in a house of thoughts. Positive thoughts encourage us and make us feel strong. Negative thoughts tear us down and make us feel weak. I'm sharing with you how YOU can use your thoughts for you instead of against you. With scientific procedure borne out into mechanical practice, apply steps one and two to harness the power of what you think about all day long. Because, as it is so infamously stated from the box office hit movie War Room, "Victories don't come by accident."

Life experiences contribute to how a paradigm is formed - good or bad.

How you were raised, a traumatic experience as a child, false teaching, and/or fables of men's traditions all led up to the person you are and the paradigm that was formed in you. If you did not intentionally align your paradigm with the truth of God's Word, then it is quite possible that you are not living your best life. To say the least, many people are not aware or do not understand that their life's circumstances are not the end of the story. Life's circumstances do not have to dictate life's outcome. You can change your life by changing not only how you think, but what you think.

Dealing with the Ugly

Sometimes in life we have to do the hard thing. One of the hardest things you will ever do is to face yourself: face the ugly things, the dark things. Face the things we wish were not there. Face the fact that sometimes we are not who people think we are. We must face the deception, the hate, the lust, and the greed. Accept the fact that the following might really be thoughts you and I have. "Am I worthy?" "I really do want the credit." I really do want my own way;" "Why was I born?" "Do I really want to live?" "Maybe if I join the crowd, then I'll be happy." "I'm not worthy of a successful life." "I hate myself." "I'm not loved." "I'm a bad person." "I will never make it." "I will always be like this." The list goes on. When we are faced with these thoughts and when these evil thoughts present themselves, half the battle is to know their source and what to do with them.

You can't deal with what you won't face. Face it, deal with it, and move on with your life.

After you face these types of thoughts, then you can deal with them. What you do with

52

them is more important than the thoughts themselves. In Matthew chapter 4, the enemy kept hurling evil and negative thoughts at Jesus. With precision as the Master, Jesus shows us exactly how to win over every thought: by using the Word of God. (This will be discussed in detail later in this book). Like most, I was condemned at the thought. I could not move past the fact that the thought was in my head. I never considered that I was not the originator of the thought. The Bible says that the enemy is the father of lies (see John 8:44) and the accuser of the brethren (see Revelation 12:10). I did not put the blame where it stood. It did not stand with me. Due to my lack of knowledge, I was not able to deal with the thoughts or appropriate them as the lies they were. Many of us face an onslaught of negative thoughts, but how we deal with them is where our power lies. Knowing is the power!

This is precisely what happened with Cain. There was a small window of opportunity for Cain to have redemption and not to follow through with what was presented to him. When the thought of killing his own brother came to him, he had a decision to make. God told him if he did well and considered wisely, then he would be accepted. Otherwise, sin was waiting at the door to have him, but he could overcome it (see Genesis 4:6-7). There we see the responsibility to follow through with good or bad thoughts lies with us. We can either deal with them with the Word of God or we can be defeated by them.

Choosing Sides

My stubbornness and my foolish pride also kept me from the freedom I was so desperately seeking—the freedom to live the life of my dreams. I thought that my old paradigm of thinking would help me to live my dream life, but it didn't work. Through my own selfish pride and arrogance, I wanted to be right, and I didn't want to change. I didn't want the answer to be in GOD. I wanted it to be like everybody said it would be. Yet, I wasn't seeing any results in my own life. I felt defeated all the time. Human, fleshly, and secular ideals that were opposite of God's Word was not the answer, "As the truth is in Jesus" (see Ephesians 4:21). It took years for me to realize that the expected cultural, familial, and the societal norms of thinking I had learned since childhood were not based on truth. What I saw on television, on the internet, and in the lives of other people was not the standard of how to create power thoughts for my own life. So, trying to create a paradigm based on truth for living from anywhere other than God's word is like trying to ride a bicycle without wheels. It just doesn't work.

Trying to fit in with human, fleshly, and secular ideals was yet another disastrous paradigm I had— keeping me from my best life. I wanted to be like everybody else. I thought that if I couldn't have the life I wanted, then at least I would, in my own way, gain their acceptance. It seemed plausible. Deep down inside it is what I wanted my whole life. I wanted to fit in, to be liked, to be admired, and not to be the odd man out. In the midst of it all, I still felt there was something missing. Trying to fit with everybody caused me to make bad decisions that separated me from GOD and the power to rid myself of negative and self-deprecating thoughts. My life was going in the opposite direction of what GOD had for me. My heart was longing for something more than secular affirmation.

> By accepting God's way and humbly submitting to His plan, I began to see the results of the life He promised me.

It was a deep longing that only my CREATOR, the God of the Universe who put Himself on a cross for me in the Person of JESUS CHRIST, could satisfy. When I humbled myself and admitted to Him, "I need you," then it all began to make sense. And every time I would go back to my old ways of thinking, things wouldn't make sense anymore. Then I realized I wasn't the only one. The Psalm of Asaph shares with us the plight of those who do not follow God's ways (see Psalms 73:1-28). I came to understand that following the crowd is not at all what it seemed.

Being uncommon, countercultural, and different, juxtaposed to current cultural norms and societal conformity, was where my peace rested. It was, and it always will be, with Him. It was Him the whole time. He was patient. In order for me to be free, I needed to maximize the freedom available to me through the blood of JESUS CHRIST and His cross. I had accepted Christ as Savior, but my mind was not free. I was bound in so many ways, and I knew it. Deliverance was available to me, but I had yet to receive it. I had yet to take it.

Once the chains of bondage are broken by Jesus and you learn what is available to you as a believer, it is the time to create the life of your dreams.

CHAPTER QUESTIONS

1. What are some ideals or experiences that helped to shape your current paradigm?

2. Which of those are opposite of God's Word?

3. Is facing your paradigm difficult for you. If so, what's worse leaving things the way they are or dealing with them to live the life of your dreams?

Chapter 6

THE COMPUTER–HUMAN MIND CONNECTION

———

The computer was fashioned after the human mind. The mind is centrally located in the brain, where thought activity takes place. This is the way I see it. To me, the brain would be the hardware of the computer and the mind would be the software. For the practical application of this book, let's compare the computer software to how the mind works. The software includes the operating system and the computer program applications loaded on to it. Comparing the software to the mind, the operating system would be considered your paradigm and the computer program applications would be your thoughts. This would be the basis of how all system components work together. The paradigm of your life would be considered your beliefs; what you accept as true or real[3]. Your thoughts include the combination of words and images that flow through your mind. Put another way, the operating system would be the "how" of the entire operation, and the thoughts would be "the what."

A computer's operating system controls the operations of the programs. The operating system will run whatever program

----

The mind will run whatever thoughts that are allowed to
stay - good or bad.

----

you upload to it. There are program applications that create
good output and program applications that create viruses and
malware. The operating system will run whatever program is
put on it. The same is with our thoughts. We will output good
results with good thoughts and bad results with bad thoughts.
The programs are the actual applications that generate
output. Thus, like the computer software that receives, stores,
processes, and generates output, so it is with the mind and
thoughts.

So, let's go back to childhood. Growing up in a loving,
happy family, where acceptance and security were the
attributes used in rearing and nurturing a child, it would be
hard for an adult to
believe that abusing
a child was normal
because that's not
how they were raised
or "programmed." On the other hand, for instance, when a
child is reared in an environment where love and acceptance
were at a deficit, they are essentially "programmed" for
rejection and fear to be normalized. Is it true? No, but that

Any childhood experience can
contribute to how you think
today.

60

is how they were programmed. Unless this individual comes into contact with a loving Savior who removes, through His power, the hurt and pain from these deficits, he or she will not have true freedom. It is called living a lie. Why? It is because the information that the person is using to make decisions and to live their lives is not based on the truth. Oftentimes, this individual will enter a relationship or work toward a goal with inherent fear or insecurity.

A Lie Versus the Truth

Being lied to, tricked, bamboozled, hoodwinked, or having the wool pulled over your eyes causes great damage, if believed. Even when it's no fault of our own, we have the responsibility for every decision we make. The greatest okie-doke in human history is to believe and take in the lie of the enemy. To accept it as truth is to use your human faculties to replicate his lies about you. For instance, if you are constantly hearing in your mind thoughts of defeat, failure, and insecurity, then that is a lie. The Word of God says we are more than conquerors through Him that loved us (see Romans 8:37). If you are constantly hearing in your mind thoughts of unworthiness, shame, or rejection, then that is a lie. The Word of God says that we are the righteousness of God in Christ Jesus (see 2 Corinthians 5:21). If you are constantly hearing thoughts in your mind of lack, poverty, and insufficiency, then it that is a lie. The Word of God says, "My God will supply all of my needs according to His riches in glory in Christ Jesus" (see Philippians 4:19). What you believe as true will be manifested in your life as long as you believe it. You believing a lie will give life and power to the lie. Conversely, you believing in the truth will give life and power to the truth. It's up to you.

Go beyond the lies and the limitations the enemy tries
to place on you.

The only one who is telling you that you can't have what God's Word promises you is the one who wants to keep you from it. You have to release yourself! Give yourself permission to go beyond limitations put on you by the enemy, your past, life's circumstances, or even people. What you believe defines you, not what happened to you. "As a man thinks in his heart, so is he" (see Proverbs 23:7). There are zero degrees (0^0) of separation between who you are and what you think. Use your power and make a decision to move past the lies, the failures, and the rejection. Delete the old operating system and old programs and reboot with a new operating system from God, allowing His Word to "program" your thoughts. Therefore, with blind faith in God's Word, let us reprogram our life as God's sees it: prosperous, in good health, even as our soul prospers (see 3 John 1:3).

A Big Myth

Another myth about the mind and our thoughts that I had to overcome is that this is mystical and it's not for Christians. It's NOT a secret. The law of attraction is the law of sowing and reaping. It comes

> Principles that we live by every day are found in the Word of GOD.

straight out of the Word of God. Scripture tells us to guard our heart, for out of it flows the issues of life (see Proverbs 4:23). This is a governing principle of how humankind was to operate in this world. We have biblical, historical, and contemporary examples of these principles working. The principles work, because those who put them into practice are operating within the guidelines of what makes the principle a principle. FACT: These principles and laws were established by GOD, also upon creation, for humans to operate within everyday life. Principles work for those who work them. Principles, rules, laws, and commandments are what govern the spiritual and physical worlds. The physical and spiritual worlds are mirrors of each other. Jesus said, "Thy Kingdom come thy will be done on Earth as it is in Heaven" (see Matthew 6:9). I like to use three references when supporting a thesis. And Jesus also said, "Whatsoever you bind on earth will be bound in heaven. Whatsoever you loose on Earth shall be loosed in Heaven" (Matthew 16:19). Be not deceived, God be not mocked, for whatsoever a man sows that shall he also reap (see Galatians 6:7). As long as the Earth remains, there shall be seedtime and harvest (see Genesis 8:22).

CHAPTER QUESTIONS

1. What experiences in your past contribute to your paradigm today?

2. How have they impacted your life's decisions?

3. Do those experience have to define you or can you move past them into newness of life from Jesus Christ?

Chapter 7

THE REAL DEAL

The Story of the Ants

If you let one evil thought come into your mind and you don't do anything about it, it becomes an open invitation for similar thoughts to come. Unabated, they will come back and invite friends. I am reminded of a pest problem I had in my home one time. One day, I saw a single black ant. It got my attention because it was 10 times the size of a regular ant, but I only saw one. I thought, *"Oh it is no big deal. I will kill it and go on about my day."* A few weeks passed, and I had not seen any more. But, in my ignorance, I did not go about dealing with the problem effectively. A couple of weeks passed, and I saw two. I followed the same procedure with the same mindset. The idea that only one or two large black ants in my house was no big deal because I could handle it was shortsighted. I killed the two and went on my way. A week later, all of a sudden, I was killing 8 ants, then 10. It became more than I could handle on my own. I had to call in for back-up. I called the exterminator. I called on someone who could fix the problem at its root. Think of this, the Word of God is the exterminator for evil thoughts.

Experiential Learning

Lessons I took from this experience:

1. There is no one isolated enemy, thought, or even ant. If you see one, then there are more. It might have been one, but that one was connected to hundreds. It was foolish of me to think that just one stray ant found its way into my house and did not leave a way for others to follow.

2. My approach to dealing with the problem was shortsighted. I dealt with one ant, but I wasn't prepared to deal with hundreds. I was not using wisdom or exercising foresight to cut off the problem before it got out of hand and out of control.

3. It was a distraction. It took me away from my work and the most effective use of my time, energy, and life's force to focus on something so seemingly insignificant that could have been avoided had I been vigilant.

That is exactly how thoughts come to counteract what we believe and for that which we live. If we don't do what the Bible teaches us and cast them down, then they will build a stronghold leading to captivity. Unchecked and not dealt with, negative thoughts and evil thoughts are like bricks. They build on top of each other and reinforce each other until they become a wall. This wall is what the Bible calls a stronghold in 2 Corinthians 10:5. Just like the ants that were overpowering me, I had to call for back-up. I couldn't destroy them one at a time anymore: they were too many for me to handle on my own. For unchecked thoughts that have become a stronghold, we need back-up. We have to call in reinforcement. The only power that can destroy strongholds in the mind is the Word of God. That is why it's so important to know it. I'm referring to knowing it intimately, with the ability to use it on command. I mean that they are not just memorized but hidden in your heart.

The weapons we use to take every thought captive come from GOD's Word.

In Ephesians 6:11-18, God gives Paul to share with believers that we have power and authority and the tools to exercise that power and authority. The tools are referred to as armor. In the battle that we win, we are instructed to put on the whole armor of God and to pray in the Spirit. We have the Breastplate of Righteousness, the Helmet of Salvation, the Belt of Truth, feet prepared with the Gospel of Peace, the Shield of Faith, the Sword of the Spirit, which is the Word of God, and prayer in the Spirit. Think about a soldier in battle fully armored. His body is covered for protection, but he also has weapons to fight. There are two weapons of which I would like to pay special attention. They are the shield and the sword. The shield quenches the fiery darts of the enemy, and the sword cuts his lies to pieces, destroying them.

Now, let's put this in practical terms. When Jesus was in the wilderness being tempted of the devil in Matthew 4, He gave us exactly how to defeat the enemy when he attacks our mind with evil thoughts. Every time the devil would try and tempt Jesus, the LORD's response was, "It is written." It is important to note that Jesus did not just pick any random scripture from the Word of God. The scriptures were very much targeted, and they were exactly the countermeasures necessary to defeat the enemy at every turn. The weapon must match the attack. In battle, if attacked with a sword, you wouldn't use a spoon to defend yourself. You would use a sword to cut off the attack. That is exactly how we use the Word of God. The Sword of the Spirit is the Word of God (see Ephesians 6:17). By using it, we are casting down imaginations, and we are taking every thought captive and bringing every thought into the obedience of Christ (see 2 Corinthians 10:5). Have you ever noticed that the scripture referenced an imagination here? The enemy's lies come in pictures and 3-D images. Cast them down. Jesus said, "The words I speak to you are spirit and they are life" (see John 6:63). If the thoughts you are hearing are not like Jesus,' you don't argue with them, you don't reason with them, and you don't agonize over them. You must make them obey

> We don't argue, we don't reason, and we don't debate evil thoughts. We do the   #1 thing; we cast them down with GOD's Word.

Christ and cast them down!

So, from our perspective, when the enemy is presenting lies about finances, it's not time for healing scriptures. I will give you an illustration of exactly how this works. He presents the lie and you quote the corresponding counterattack from the Holy Scriptures! Use the example below as a strategy to counter the lies of the enemy. Be very precise in the execution of this strategy. When the enemy presents lies like those listed below, say out loud the following scriptures. I will provide some examples of the lies of the enemy and corresponding scriptures to use to counter them. For example:

We do like Jesus did in Matthew Chapter 4 say, "It is written...."

Lie of the enemy	Confessions of Counterattack to Cast Down the Lies of the enemy
"You're a nobody."	I am the righteousness of God in Christ Jesus (see 2 Corinthians 5:21)
	I am chosen, a royal priesthood, a holy nation (see I Peter 2:9).
	I am a king and priest unto God (see Revelations 1:6).
"You'll die sick."	He Himself bore my infirmities by whose stripes I was healed (see I Peter 2:24)

71

| He was wounded for my transgressions, bruised for my iniquities: the chastisement of my peace was upon Him; and with his stripes I am healed (see Isaiah 53:5).

| I will live and not die and declare the works of the LORD (see Psalms 118:17).

"You're depressed." | Peace I leave with you, my peace I give unto you: not as the world giveth, I give unto you. Let not your heart be troubled, neither let it be afraid (see John 14:27).

Thou wilt keep him in perfect peace, whose mind is stayed on thee: because he trusteth in thee (see Isaiah 26:3).

And the peace of God, which passeth all understanding, shall keep your hearts and minds through Christ Jesus (see Philippians 4:7).

"You are defeated" | I am more than a conqueror through Him who loves me (see Romans 8:37).

| Thanks be to God who gives me the victory (see 1 Corinthians 15:57).

| Thanks be to God who always causes me to triumph in Christ (see 2 Corinthians 2:14).

"You'll always be poor" | It is God who gives me the power to get wealth to establish His covenant (See Deuteronomy 8:18).

| God supplies all of my needs according to His riches in glory Christ Jesus (see Philippians 4:19).

| The blessing of the LORD makes one rich and He adds no sorrow with it see Proverbs 10:22).

From where do you think your life comes? It's what you make of it every single day. Thoughts have a counterpart in real-time.

Thoughts create 100% of the time and I am in control of my thoughts 100% of the time.

Your life is a sum total of the thoughts you decided to think. Every thought that you think is a building block for your everyday life. It's not about what he did or what she did. It's not about what he said or she said. You are 100% responsible for how your life turns out. You get out of your life exactly what you put into it. No matter what may have happened in your past, Jesus has the power to free you from it, to create from the ashes of it and make your life beautiful. But, he needs your participation. What goes up must come down. Goodness goes in and goodness comes out. Garbage goes in and garbage comes out. What goes in the system and what comes out of the system are not mutually exclusive. They work hand in hand.

Think about it this way, the thoughts you've had for many years are a reflection of your life right now. Thoughts have a counterpart in real-time. Say this to yourself, "My reality is equivalent to my thoughts." I believe this is true, therefore _____ happened. You fill in the blank. I believe this is true like I believed that was true. Looking at the illustration below, there is no other determining factor between thinking lies and thinking the truth of God's Word other than making the choice between the two of them.

Illustration

Lies   Truth

<------------ me -------------->

Fear   Faith

Dominating Thoughts

What is the deciding factor in your life's whole dynamic? You! Whichever one you believe and think about is the one that will be activated. All things are possible to them that believe (see Mark 9:23). Whatever you believe, that is what's possible for you. You are the sum total of your thoughts! PERIOD. The scripture says, "As a man thinks in his heart so is he" (see Proverbs 23:7). You cannot be something outside of what you think. Your life will never be greater than the magnitude of your most dominant thought.

You think you're a winner; you are right. You think you're a failure; you are right. The decision is yours. You have been bestowed with the power to do your part in the creative process of life. Your life situation cannot and will not change until you decide to do something about it. Even at salvation, you have to accept the calling of the LORD. Then, He does the saving. It's that basic. It takes the adversary to overcomplicate it, making it seem confusing. It is not. Think it, see it. PERIOD. Focusing on the impossible magnifies the impossibility. Focusing on the limitless possibilities magnifies limitless possibilities.

The mentality, mindset, paradigm, thoughts, that you think shows up in your life in real-time. You may wonder, why, if *I give, confess, pray, and do right by others, has my life not changed?* Things have not changed because you have not given your life any new instructions on what to create. You always think about your past. Your yesterday dominates your life. What happened to you, what you did wrong, uninformed decisions you have made, and who hurt you engulfs your every thought, not to mention the news you watch, the social media you pay attention to, or to whom you listen. It all matters because it all is going into your mind.

> Whether you think you will win or you think you will lose, you are right.

Like the computer, the mind's job is to take in information and to store in for future use generating output. If that's not the direction you want your life to go, then why allow it into your mind? Not one of those things has anything to do with creating the life of your dreams.

By constantly focusing on your past or negative and insulting news, you relive it every day. You can be stuck. How do you get unstuck? Think new thoughts. Change what you watch; redirect your attention from negative people and listen to good news. Train your mind to think happy thoughts. Reliving the past is like eating leftovers over and over again. Even after they spoil, some people still eat them, and that's from where sickness and depression come.

> What you focus on expands and gets bigger and bigger.

There is nothing that can convince me to change my mind about what I want and the life I want to live. I made a conscious, intentional, and deliberate decision, as an act of my God-given will, to live the life God promised me. I set the goal; I pursue the target until I get it. I accept it as possible. Therefore, it's possible. Becoming one with the promise is evidence and proof that I have what I believe will come to reality. That is where my life gets the information to simulcast what I believe and manifest its material counterpart in real-time. It's what I have already accepted and received as mine. That's taking it. That is the essence of faith—my thinking congruent with my believing. What I have come to realize is that thinking is an actionable force that is a key ingredient in creating my everyday life.

Should've, could've, would've are all a waste of mental energy. All of these self-imposed restrictions, old wives' tales, traditions of men, are flat out lies of the enemy. They are all destiny-blockers that we as humans erroneously engage when the Bible gives us one instruction. I don't wrestle with them. I don't argue with them. I don't reason with them. I don't debate them. I cast them down. If thoughts come to me that do not line up with the Word of God about my life, I do one thing. I cast them down. PERIOD. I reject them and speak the truth of the promises of God to me.

CHAPTER QUESTIONS

1. What are some of your most dominate thoughts?

2. Have they helped or hindered you to reaching your goals?

3. What are your favorite scriptures that help you to lead a victorious life?

Chapter 8

CHANGE THE TAPE

Think on these things....

If you want new output in your life, then you must have new input from the old in your mind. Change the tape! Change your thought patterns that are producing negative results to positive thought patterns for positive results by changing what you think about. The Bible says, "As a man thinks in his heart so is he" (see Proverbs 23:7). To reprogram the mind is to change the paradigm. Your paradigm is the operating system that is the foundation for who you are and what you believe. These are your core values and your guiding principles. The thoughts we think are like the programs. As followers of Jesus Christ, we receive our core values and guiding principles from His Word. The thoughts we think determine the outcome of what is in our life. If "as a man thinks in his heart, then so is he" and we are to "guard our heart; for out of it flows the issues of our life," then it stands to reason that what

> A man is what he thinks about all day long.
> -Norman Vincent Peale

flows in the thoughts flows into our lives. If your paradigm is positive, then your thoughts will be positive. If your paradigm is negative, then your thoughts will be negative.

"Finally, brethren, whatsoever things *are* true, whatsoever things *are* honest, whatsoever things *are* just, whatsoever things *are* pure, whatsoever things *are* lovely, whatsoever

---

Life by design requires intentionality of your thoughts and what you think about on a consistent basis.

---

things *are* of good report; if *there* be any virtue, and if *there* be any praise, think on these things" (see Philippians 4:8). This new life by design takes practicality and intentionality. There are real life day-to-day action steps that must be taken in order to actualize the life you desire. It doesn't happen by happenstance. I have what I like to call "go-to thoughts." I sat down and made a list of all the things I like to think about that make me happy: things that are productive and that contribute to the life I want to live. These are thoughts that I can think about all day long. When negative thoughts come, I switch to thinking of things on my list. Take a moment and take out a sheet of paper. On the left side write the words true, honest, just, pure, lovely, good report, virtue, and praise. On the right side, write down things that correspond to those words that you can think about. For example, see below:

THE THINGS	THE THOUGHTS
True	God is love. Jesus died for me. I'm alive today to receive God's goodness.
Honest	A baby's eyes
Just	Winning the game from hard work and preparation
Pure	A mother's love
Lovely	A bouquet of flowers, a gentle spring rain, a rainbow, birds chirping
Good Report	I passed the test, I got the promotion, and a stranger received salvation today
Virtue	Helping others and seeing their joy
Praise	GOD for His Grace

It may take a minute to orient your mind to this new way of

thinking, but it does work. It worked for me. The more you do this, the more it will work. The more you flood your mind with positive thoughts; the negative thoughts get weaker and weaker. Back to our computer analogy, when too many programs are going on at one time, the mind, like the computer, will

> Sitting down and thinking about what you are thinking about is key to living a life of 100% victory.

slow down. When the system gets too overwhelmed, with fragmented pieces of information, requests, commands, or too overheated, it will shut down. When the operating system is so old that it no longer supports the new software, a new operating system is required. This is why it is imperative that you are single-minded in what you feed your mind. In the book of James, it tells us that a double-minded man is unstable in all his ways and he can't receive anything from the LORD (see James 1:6-8). Right, wrong, or indifferent, your thoughts create your reality. A helpful tip: to keep good in your life, keep good on your mind. To keep bad out of your life, keep bad off your mind.

Keeping your mind set on the correct mindset comes from a predetermined strategy and list of "go-to" thoughts.

The goal is to have the life that you want. In order for this to occur, your thoughts must be in order. As with the computer, the programs or applications are like our thoughts. They determine the output. So, if what we believe is true (the paradigm) is controlling our thoughts (the programs or applications), then the resulting outcome of our life can be no different than the information that was generated. What goes into the system will come out of the system. It is how God designed it to be. It is the output of the applications that generates the answers and the results we seek. This in turn gives us our behaviors, our decisions, our actions, and our words. It's just like how the computer gives us new outputs of information, calculations, answers, designs, code, etc.

Just as Jesus said, you can't put new wine in old wine skins. If you do, the wineskins that are old cannot support the weight of the new wine and it spills all over the ground (see Matthew 9:17). By establishing what old beliefs and thoughts we must

Always keep your mind on what is...

- Good
- Right and
- True (see Eph. 5:8-9)

rid ourselves of, we begin to redefine the direction of our lives. This process begins to reshape our lives, because our thoughts have been reshaped. So, things that are true, honest, just, pure, lovely, of good report, virtuous, or worthy of praise all become the masterful ingredients that shape the life we want.

We reshape our lives as our thoughts are reshaped with God's Word. We go around and around in circles trying to figure out why things are not working. It's because we have faulty operating systems and programming live by unconsciously. Negative experiences have the tendency to shape a mindset. If I was offended, skipped over, abused, abandoned, or rejected, then it might open the door for that narrative to

---

Make the Shift - Change the Tape

---

shape a negative self-image. All of these experiences were designed to try and convince me that I am not what I believe. So often, not only do we have an outdated program operating system, but our "computer" has a virus—a malicious code in the program designed to sabotage the optimal operating output of life and life more abundantly. You have to rid the old information to prepare for the new information and the new output. In order to create new applications and new possibilities, reprogram the tape from a negative to a positive mentality. Create a mindset that shifts from "I can't" to "I can", from doubt to faith, from failure to success, from no to yes, from impossibility to possibility, from denied to granted, from rejected to accepted, and from fear to love.

Whatever you believe, that is what is possible for you.

Back to the computer analogy, information that you heard, things you have experienced, things you've seen, and things you've read were all stored in your memory to be retrieved for later use. You either accepted or rejected them as truth; creating your beliefs. This regulated what comes in and out of your life. For example, if a person is an agoraphobic, thinking that they are going to be harmed if they leave their home, then they never leave their home. They are acting on what they think and believe, even though millions of people every day leave their home for work, school, church, errands, lunch with their friends, or a date with their spouse. Because they think that they will be harmed, that is what is possible to them. They are limited to this stronghold of thinking and thus have subjugated their lives to it.

As you recall, the spiritual world and the physical world mirror each other. Thus, it is the same with our thoughts. Every thought that comes into your mind is there working for you or against you. Your power comes in when you know what to do with each. There is no such thing as that thought doesn't matter. Every thought matters. Repeat after me, "Every thought matters!" Thoughts are things. Thoughts create. Thoughts are the infrastructure of what your life is built upon. That is why the Bible tell us to

> Every thought counts.
>
> Every thought counts.
>
> Every thought counts.

"Guard your heart for out of it flows the issues of life" (see Proverbs 4:23). It is because the thoughts are the bridge between the physical and spiritual worlds. They make up the difference between the natural and the supernatural, the manifested and the unmanifested worlds. You can activate thoughts both with spiritual things and natural things. For instance, belief transmutes into thoughts that transfers into actions. Thoughts are the agents that create change. Thoughts precede words. Thoughts precede actions. Thoughts are the vehicle from the unseen to the seen, with its physical equivalent.

CHAPTER QUESTIONS

1. What are some of your most dominate thoughts?

2. Have they helped or hindered you to reaching your goals?

3. What are your favorite scriptures that help you to lead a victorious life?

Chapter 9

THE SCIENTIST'S PERSPECTIVE

Every Thought Matters and Here's Why

The power of positive thinking is the one true way to create the life that you want: a life of maximum power over every ill that life brings. Life creates after its own kinds just as water seeks its own level. So too will life create after the information you put in it. In the scientific world, there is a law that governs that physical world that is so relevant when it comes to understanding spiritual principles. It is the First Law of Thermodynamics[4].

$$\Delta EUniverse = \Delta ESurroundings + \Delta ESurroundings = 0$$

This means all energy is accounted for. Again, what goes into the system comes out of the system. The same goes for physical matter. The Law of Conservation of Matter indicates that matter is neither created nor destroyed, but conserved[5]. For example, whether you are writing a chemical equation for water or you're baking a cake, the principle is still the same. What goes in the system must come out of the system and must be accounted for. Writing the balanced chemical equation for hydrogen and oxygen equaling water is as follows:

$$2H_2 + O_2 = 2H_2O$$

Why would you not expect zinc, aluminum, or potassium to be after the equal sign? You wouldn't expect it because it was not there before the equal sign.

This plus this equals that. It's that simple.

Now would you expect broccoli to appear in your baked cake that you used flour and water to make if you didn't put it there? So, why would you think that you could think on negative, self-deprecating thoughts and have a productive and successful life? Additionally, why would you think you can take in negative, scary, angry, hate-filled, and negative media consistently and live a beautiful and peaceful life? Beauty coming out of your life is only the result of beauty going into your life. Just as gravity falls at 9.8 m/s^2, the law which governs creation in our world works just like clockwork. Your thoughts create 100% of the time.^{SM} It's that's simple.

It took our adversary to convolute this life maxim to the point of being impalpable. When in actuality, it can be borne out by scientific procedure in mechanical practice. The type of life you want takes intentional step-by-step, deliberate practices. It's that easy. The thoughts you think create the life around you. The words you speak reinforce the thoughts you think in this creative process. What you believe is the fundamental ingredient. The interconnected mind-heart-ears-mouth system God instituted is what makes us different from any other species on this planet. We have the power and ability to use our human faculties to create. The mind uses thoughts to create. The thoughts are the fundamental packets of light energy which are actually things. Thoughts are things! They are carriers of the material that turn potential to possibility. The mind is like the factory where thoughts are generated, stored, packaged, and sent out.

"You create your life from the canvas of your imagination."

Whenever God wants to teach me something, He asks me a question. One day, the Holy Spirit spoke to my heart and said, "What's in the container?" I interpreted that as, "What's on your mind?" "What are you thinking about?" It is often said that what you focus on gets bigger and stronger. That is when I realized that I kept meditating on the lies of who the enemy said I was. This created a vicious cycle of defeat. It was then that the Holy Spirit confirmed to me that, **"You create your life from the canvas of your imagination.**^{SM}**"** That is when I realized that I was the one recreating what I was hearing from the enemy. I then became really vigilant about what I was thinking about while driving, cooking, or working on a task. I became very intentional about what was playing on the "tape" of my mind. I started visualizing me in the promise of God over my life, thinking about scriptures, and praising and worshipping God.

Blank Canvas

You see, your mind is a blank canvas until you put something on it. Your life is based on what you see with your mind's eye. The only things your life can and will produce is what you feed it or what you draw on the canvas. How you see yourself is the determining factor of what your life will generate and bring back to you. The law of sowing and reaping is the law which regulates what to do with what type of thoughts the mind generates. Bob Proctor says that, "The brain is an electronic switching station" on which all of the interactions of electrical energy activity occur"[6]. The mind is the non-material space where creative activity occurs.

You will hear something negative over and over again, and that thing creates an image, an imagination. If you don't do something with it, it may very well become a stronghold. That is why the Scripture tells us to "Cast down every imagination and every high thing that lifts itself against the knowledge of God and lead every thought away captive into the obedience of Christ" (see 2 Corinthians 10:5). The Word tells us that the accuser of the brethren has been cast down (see Revelations 12:9). The liar wants to lie to us over and over again. We have to actually do something to counter those lying thoughts or those thoughts will manifest into our very lives and their physical counterparts. If he is lying about depression and we don't counter those thoughts, then depression can show up. The list goes on.

We counter thoughts with words: the WORD. That's what JESUS did. We follow His example.

The Holy Spirit gave me a way to remember what to do when negative thoughts come to my mind. He said, "Evil thoughts come from an outlaw spirit." What do we do with outlaws that don't obey the laws? We lock them up. So, thoughts that come to my mind that do not line up with the WORD of GOD and obey Christ, I lock up and cut to pieces with what God's Word says about me. That is why it is so important to read the Bible, to memorize scripture, and quote verses to yourself so that you can be ready and on guard when the enemy comes. Jesus is the Word of God. He is the same Word that was made flesh and dwelt among us in St. John 1. The Word made the worlds in Genesis. Revelations 19:11-21 tells us that Jesus, The Word of God, won the ultimate battle. We use the selfsame Word to create our world and to defeat the enemy.

> Counter lying thoughts with the Truth of the Word of GOD.

CHAPTER QUESTIONS

1. Do you expect a life of lies and intimidating thoughts to produce positive results?

2. What strategy is used to help with imagining and creating the life of your dreams?

3. What does the scripture instruct us to do when negative, evil, or self-deprecating thoughts come?

PART 3

Thoughts Create

Chapter 10

Now It's Time for You to Create

Out with Old and in with the New

This is where the fun starts! Now your mind is free and clear. Now your mind is free to create! This is when your soul begins to sour. Your mind and your thoughts are free to create your wildest dreams and turn them into the life you live in real-time. Your mind and your consciousness align fully with GOD's Word in a pre-fall state. How do you think it was possible for Adam to name *all* the animals? His creative thought was free of sin-consciousness and judgment from sin. I can turn my mind in the direction I want my life to go and cultivate it with corresponding thoughts. Ultimately, what it boiled down to was that I have to listen to and hear, and hear, and hear, over and over again, the information that is true—The Word of God. I have to technically convince myself that what God said about me is the Truth and what they enemy had been barraging me with, the mental assaults of false information, was actually a lie. Identified in this section are practical habits that you can develop. They will help you to be able to identify self-defeating thoughts and what to do with them.

Once Jesus has broken any chain of bondage or stronghold, it's time for you to create! Remember, you are what you think. "As a man thinks in his heart, so is he" (see Proverbs 23:7). There is no degree of separation from that scripture and

---

Your most dominate thoughts are your current paradigm. Change the paradigm and the thoughts and you change your life.

---

the reality of your life right now. Take a moment and write down the ten most prevalent thoughts you have on a day-to-day basis and reflect. To the degree you think, is the degree your life shall be. Much of the results in our lives are not spiritual. Think about it. Why would God put us on planet Earth, living in a physical body governed by physical laws, if we were to dictate the outcomes of our lives from a spiritual perspective? Jesus took care of our spiritual salvation on the cross. Now it is time to do our part. The funny thing is that non-believers have harnessed this power. But it's not spiritual in nature. If they have not accepted Jesus Christ as their LORD and Savior, they will have obtained everything they wanted in this life with their thoughts and miss out on Heaven. As a believer, we get both: our reward now and in the life to come (see Mark 10:29-30).

The Life of a Butterfly

Like a butterfly, your soul is free and has transformed to do what it was created to do—to soar. A butterfly that starts out as a caterpillar was not meant to be grounded to the Earth or trees; it was meant to fly. It is our innate ability as a created being, created in GOD's image and likeness, to create. All of this is borne out in the first book of the Bible: Genesis. First, GOD says it in Genesis 1:26. But, the story of our creative ability is actually given light in Genesis 11:6: "And the LORD said, Behold the people is one, and they have all one language; and this they begin to do: and now nothing will be restrained from them, which they have imagined to do." Continuity and focus are the foundation of strength and momentum. All of their energy going in the same direction would provide them the power to create whatever they imagined. We must laser in on our thoughts and be intentional to use our thoughts to see the life that we want just as the people in Genesis chapter 11 did.

Say it Loud

To have the life that you want, you have to watch your thoughts. There is intentionality and a focus that is involved. "Guard you heart with all diligence for out of it flows the issues of life" (see Proverbs 4:20-23). The life you want is waiting for you...to create it! Repeat after me, "I have the power within me to create the life that I was created to live. My dream is God's dream for me. By the very nature that it is in my heart to live a better life, it is what God wants for me too."

Doubt, fear, and unbelief are a bandit trio. They steel

> By paying attention to what you pay attention to, you are being intentional with your thoughts.

focus, energy, and momentum to create. Think of it this way. If your mind was like a factory and what you put into it created some widget as a product, then a healthy body, a successful family, financial freedom, deliverance, a loving marriage, and peace are what you should be thinking about. Doubt, fear, and unbelief would jam the factory systems and no products would come out. It is absolutely true that our thoughts create 100% of the time. It is a law that GOD instituted when HE ordained our lives to be governed by laws of the spiritual and physical worlds.

The function of our thoughts used to create our life is in supernatural alignment with our God-likeness.[SM] That is what the mind of Christ is for, to return us back to our true identity before the fall. Genesis 11:9 bears this out beautifully.

We were created to be in the likeness of GOD and nothing our enemy or the nature of sin can change that.

Jesus came to show us how to operate as spiritual beings living in a natural body. So, if I am being attacked by an evil spirit, all the positive thinking in the world and affirmations will not stop it. I use the power and the authority of the name of JESUS CHRIST, because demon spirits are not afraid of, and neither are they subject to, human thoughts. They are only subject to the power and authority of JESUS CHRIST in you—the Word. He has all authority and power. Jesus said "All POWER has been given unto me both in Heave and Earth" (see Matthew 28:18). And He gave that same power to you and me: "Behold I give unto you power, over all the power of the enemy and nothing shall by any means hurt you" (see Luke 10:19). You see, the finished work of the cross of Christ gave us the same power. We are complete in Him who is the head of all principality and power (see Colossians 2:10-14).

Now, my spirit-man needs strength and building up to relate to God and to have authority over the enemy in the spiritual world. My psychological and emotional inner man needs strength and building up to create my life, my world

> We have power and authority to cast down every thought that does not line up with the Word of GOD.

around me. The truth is I am a creative being. GOD made me that way. The moment I was born my creative ability began. The creativity I'm referring to is not that of artists or musicians (although it can translate to that later in life). I am talking about my GOD-given ability to direct my thoughts, to create, to the end of the physical manifestation of my thoughts. Jesus said, "ALL things are possible to them that believe" (Mark 9:23). He revealed to me the human psychological aspect of that scripture. It is whatever you believe that is what is possible for you. I am the operator, the director, the controller, and the creator of what is to be manifested around me in real-time.

The Story of Life

I came to realize that life is an open system. What I hear, what I see, and accept as truth in my heart makes up what I believe. What I believe works with my heart to create in my life, in real-time, what my heart has accepted as truth, fact, or reality. GOD essentially gave me the tools to build His Kingdom and to live a heavenly life here on Earth by my volition, intentionally, and consciousness, using my thoughts to create. That is how we accept Jesus into our life. By what we believe, think, and speak! Romans 10:10 says, "With the heart man believes unto righteousness and with the mouth confession is made unto salvation." Verse 17 tells us, "So then faith comes by hearing and hearing by the Word of GOD." On the flip side, so does fear.

If the enemy of your soul has said to you over and over again that you are afraid of spiders, YOU have the power at the moment to accept or reject that as truth, fact, or reality. At the switch, you had the power to accept or reject it. Remember, the computer was modeled after the human mind. The mind was created by God to take in information to store in and

> What I believe works with my heart to create in my life, in real-time, what my heart has accepted as truth, fact, or reality.

process it for future use. If you do not do something with the information that you hear and it is saved in your memory, then the computer or mind will use it for output, i.e. your reactions. So, guess what? If you did not strip those words of their power and you allow them to be saved in your memory, when your eyes see spiders, the mind will trigger fear. By listening to good material, journaling, reading God's Word and, to the extent possible, eliminating negative information, you can shift your entire mentality to one of peace and success.

I am loved by a Good GOD and my paradigm is shaped around His love for me and my expected end.

It took years of lies, disappointments, hurt, rejection, and painful experiences to shape the narrative of "Why would God do anything for you?" This is the lie of the enemy. Therefore, it takes much work and intentionality to delete the program and reboot to the following truths: God loves me. I am successful. God is good, and I accept the fact that He wants good for me. Jesus came that I might have life and have it more abundantly (see John 10:10). It will take work. How well you want your new life to take shape will depend on the diligence, repetition, perseverance, patience, and determination you put in to creating and living the life you have always dreamed. Once, you thought on death, tragedy, calamity, sickness, failure and negativity. NOW, you have to reflect on limitlessness, possibility, positivity, goodness, success, growth, access, permission, approval, affirmation, acceptance, love, honor, favor, forgiveness, health, wholeness, and the list goes on.

Chapter Questions

1. What is your new mindset about your dream life?

2. What scripture helps you to know you have power over the enemy?

3. What makes me to be in alignment with my God-likeness?

Chapter 11

AND... ACTION!!

L et's settle it today. There will be no more back and forth. Choose to be successful and deal with opportunities for improvement. We live with no doubt (see James 1:6). If you doubt, then you self- disqualify what you think, speak, and believe. We can experience an event so traumatic in our life that the wires to switch on our creative faculties could be damaged. Or, we could have been exposed to spiritual darkness and its chains of bondage that only Jesus can break. When you really think what you desire is going to happen, you take actionable steps to get it accomplished. This is as natural as breathing, and it works like clockwork. Try it!

Taking action is really about knowing and owning the fact that you can take steps to life out the Promises of GOD in your life.

Let's say, for example, you make a decision to drive to the store to purchase groceries. Think about the actionable steps that are required to drive to the store for the purpose of purchasing groceries. Also, think about the accomplished decisions you made and write them down on one side of a sheet of paper. Now, make a list of all of the things that could possibly stop you from driving to the store right now. Which one of those is out of your control? Let's examine them. If you lose your keys, then you could find them. If you're out of gas, then you call AAA. If a boulder from the mountain from behind your home falls into your driveway, then you would take an Uber. If you fall and break your leg and are unable to leave your home, then you could call Instacart to get your items for you. I'm being a bit playful here, but you get my point. The only difference between people who live their dreams and those who do not, is that the people who live their dreams believe that they can and take the necessary steps to accomplish them.

We have examples in nature that teaches us the power of learned behavior.

Looking at learned behavior

The GOD-given ability to create, centered on your thoughts, can be seen in nature. I'm reminded of the story of the flies in the jar. Two different sets of flies were in two separate jars with lids. Flies in jar #1 flew out once the lid was removed. Flies in jar #2 tried to fly out of the jar but bounced right back down off the lid. Every time the flies tried to escape jar #2, they would hit the lid of the jar. This happened repeatedly until they no longer tried to escape jar #2 even when the lid was removed. The flies flew up to the level of the lid and never beyond. Why? It is because repeated failure "programmed" them for failure, prohibiting their natural right to fly free. So it is with our lives. We were born to be free, and repeated negative information and experiences can prohibit us from this freedom.

Let's look at other animals in the animal kingdom that are of lesser intelligence but use their instincts to accomplish their tasks. Grasshoppers leverage the wind to get as far away as 200 times their body weight. Ants leverage the strength of other ants. Bees leverage the work ethic of other bees. All of these examples reveal resilience with limitlessness and possibility. When you get to the place where life can't tell you no, then there is no limit, and there is no impossibility. Think about the childhood story of the little engine that could. He kept saying to himself, "I think I can. I think I can." That is how we must think.

I remember hearing a saying that goes like this, "whether you think you can or think you can't, you're right." You are the machine! You control the input, and you control the output. Just like a computer. YOU want a different output, YOU delete the old program-PARADIGM and YOU reinstall! I would like to share a poem that captivates the tenor of this written work.

The Man Who Thinks He Can
Poem by Walter D. Wintle[7]

If you think you are beaten, you are;

If you think you dare not, you don't;

If you'd like to win, but think you can't,

It's almost a cinch you won't.

If you think you'll lose, you're lost,

For out in the world we find

Success begins with a fellow's will,

It's all in the state of mind.

If you think you're outcasted, you are;

You've got to think high to rise.

You've got to be sure of yourself before

You can ever win a prize.

Life's battles don't always go

To the stronger or faster man;

But soon or late[r] the man who wins

Is the man who thinks he can.

Here is another:

I Bargained with Life for a Penny
By Jesse B. Rittenhouse[8]

I bargained with Life for a penny,

And Life would pay no more,

However I begged at evening

When I counted my scanty store;

For Life is a just employer,

He gives you what you ask,

But once you have set the wages,

Why, you must bear the task.

I worked for a menial's hire,

Only to learn, dismayed,

That any wage I had asked of Life,

Life would have paid.

Every day you wake up is a new day to create. So, every day you wake up is a day of visualization, not rehashing all of the old memories of what did not go right, who left you, or who said what. That creates a cycle of sludge that keeps you stuck.

> Every day you wake is a day to create.

The only way to create the new cycle of the life you want is to forget those things which are behind and reach forward to those things which are before (see Philippians 3:13). One of the ways the Holy Spirit helped me to understand how important thoughts are in connection to the life I was living was by giving me this saying: "What's in you will come out of you, and what comes out of you will come to you." This is the law of attraction based on scripture. "Be not deceived, God be not mocked, for whatsoever a man sows that shall he also reap" (see Galatians 6:7). He also asked me, "What's in the container?" He was referring to what I think about on a continuous basis. Repeat after me, "The power is within me to CREATE the life that I want! The life that I have always wanted is waiting for me...to CREATE it!"

As mentioned earlier, God made reference to the power of man's ability to create on his own volition in Genesis chapter 11. The people had decided to build a tower. The decision was key. The power of the unified focus of a people to create something they imagined that would reach beyond the sky was next. This was a very clear indication in scripture that with focus and imagination, nothing is impossible. The major mistake I made was underestimating my own ability to imagine. I underestimated the power of my own thoughts. You see, it does not matter how others see you. It depends on how you see yourself. I

> Never underestimate the power of your own thoughts.

allowed how my enemy saw me to dictate how I saw myself. I opened the gateway and allowed his view of me, his limitations, his fear, his doubt, failure, and other negatives of life to be superimposed on my thought system. This is a huge no-no. The enemy has multiple weapons to try and use against us. The enemy can use people as well. It does not matter who it is. It could be the people closest to you: your family, your friends, the people you love the most, someone you hold in high regard or high esteem, or someone you admire or respect. What I learned was that sabotage to living the life that you want is allowing other people's opinion of you, ideas of how your life should be, and the voice of negativity to become louder and greater than your very own voice. Regardless of the source of the negative input, you must deal with it. Your decision and your permission are required to let this negative input take affect and try and stop you from creating. It's all up to you to not let it happen.

CHAPTER QUESTIONS

1. What is stopping you from choosing to think the right thoughts? Is any-thing?

2. What motivates you to think thoughts that are congruent with the life of your dreams?

3. What can we glean from the poems listed above?

Chapter 12

IMAGINE THAT!

As mentioned in the previous chapter, our imagination has tremendous power. Our imagination is the light that guides us to the life that we are moving toward. In order to maximize every day that you are gifted

> You create your life from the canvas of your imagination.

with, you must be intentional on using your thoughts, every given moment, to create. See yourself as you want to become, visualize where you want to be, daydream about what a day in your future reality looks like. Your imagination and your subconscious mind are blueprints for the life you intentionally create, and your thoughts are the transmitter to make it happen. The Holy Spirit said to me, **"You create your life from the canvas of your imagination.**^{SM}**"** When you intentionally and irrevocably decide to live the life that you want, you systematically take actions to get there. One day you are there in your mind, before you know it you will be there in real-time. Once you have put all the pillars in place to start creating your life, you must develop new thought patterns. There is a new modius operandi: a new operating system, new thoughts, new habits, new words, new visions, and new beliefs which are all congruent with what you are creating. Make sure you write your vision. Create a vision board. Take time to sit and visualize yourself doing what you dream and what you love.

Setting the target, is making the decision.

It's not overly complicated. You set a target—decide. Okay, let's talk eggs. You go into the kitchen and look in the refrigerator, and there are no eggs. Then, you make plans to get eggs. You have to get in your car and drive to a grocery store to buy the eggs. You get in the car, but you realized you have a flat tire. You call roadside assistance and wait for them to come to put air in your tire. You start driving to the grocery store. On your way there, you hear sirens; traffic is backed up. You perceive that there is an accident. So, instead of sitting in traffic, you take a detour. You drive around the stalled traffic to get to your eggs. You arrive at the grocery store. It took you a little longer, but that's okay. You are there. You get a grocery cart and proceed to the dairy section. You get there, and they're out of eggs. Instead of leaving the store without your eggs, you ask the grocer if there are any more eggs in stock. He goes to the back and, after a few minutes, he comes and tells you the delivery truck was stalled but is on its way. You walk around the grocery store and realize you need fruit, flour, and butter for your breakfast to go with your eggs. You wanted to make good use of your time while you wait. The grocer finds you on the baking aisle and hands you a fresh carton of eggs. Not only did waiting give you the best, freshest eggs possible, but also you were able to get other things that you needed.

This is how life is. The will of God and the divine purpose of God are the only things that could possibly redirect you: providing safety, guidance, and protection along the way to your destiny. You have a part to play, and God will back you

----

As humans, we partner with GOD to create the life HE promised us we would live.

----

up. In Matthew 16:19 Jesus says, "Whatsoever you bind, I'll bind. Whatsoever you loose, I'll loose." "All things work together for good for them who love God and who are called according to His purpose" (see Romans 8:28). Just as the empty fridge, flat tire, accident on the road, un-stocked dairy sections, or a delayed delivery truck wouldn't stop you from your eggs, so it is with your God-given goals and dreams. Delay is not denial. This thing called life, with its ups and downs and twists and turns, "works in us a far more exceeding weight of glory" (See 2 Corinthians 4:17).

If the thief is intentional about lying to you every day from

Sun up to Sun down, then make it a point to counter his lies with the Word of God. There are actual rules of engagement when it comes to the intentionality of pursuing the promises of God for your life. The cardinal rule is to renew your mind to what God says in HIS Word (see Romans 12:1-3). Rehearse it over and over again just like the thief rehearses lies in your mind. The thoughts of negativity actually made a place, a home, and stronghold in my mind. I had to do something to remove them.

Rehearsing the word
of God over and over
not only eradicated

Change the tape.

the lies of the enemy, but also set up a new paradigm for the life I was getting ready to live. This is with scientific procedure borne out in mechanical practices. I did this religiously; I played it in my mind with repetition at least three times per day, if not more. Well, you might ask, "What do I rehearse?"

It looks like this:

I rehearsed: What the Holy Spirit spoke to my heart

I rehearsed: What was spoken through someone HE sent to me

I rehearsed: What HE said in HIS Word—the Holy Scripture

Power Thoughts from Scripture with the Corresponding Action

1. Renew your mind (see Romans 12:1-3).

2. Cast down bad thoughts with God's Word (see 2 Corinthians 10:5).

3. Think positively and don't think negatively. Find something positive to think about…(see Philippians 4:8).

4. Make a declaration that whatever you believe is possible for you (see Mark 9:23).

5. Make a determination that you will not go back and forth with what you think and what you believe. (see James 1:8).

How you see yourself is most powerful

See yourself healed. That's a good thing to think about. See your marriage blessed. That's a good thing to think about. See your children saved and serving the LORD. Thoughts create, and they are very powerful. They connect to their physical counterpart in real-time. My thoughts said things wouldn't happen, and they didn't. Now my thoughts say things can happen and they do, just like I thought they would. Let me give you an example.

An example of this book in action

In 2016, I wanted a book deal. I was college professor. I had published my dissertation, and I wanted to write a book on the cross-section of how critical thinking, creativity, and innovation were the foundations of science, technology, engineering, and mathematics (S.T.E.M.) in the 21st century. I was sitting in my office one day, and I said out loud and with finality, "I am going to get a book deal." I googled where publishers meet every year. I learned it was at the world's largest publishing convention: BookExpo America in Chicago. I found a round-trip airline ticket to Chicago on sale for $58. That was my first sign. Then, I called my Dad, who is now retired, to determine if he would like to go with me. He said yes and mentioned that he had a friend who lived in Chicago who wouldn't mind a stay-over visit. That was sign number two. I prepared my first chapter, business cards, and booked a rental car. I entered the McCormick Center with my mind made up that I was not leaving Chicago without a book deal. With my elevator pitch ready, I spoke of my book to everyone I met. I ran into another author who loved my idea and shared it with her publisher. One meeting led to another. Needless to say, I left Chicago with a book deal. Think. Create. Innovate.| S.T.E.M. was published. That's how I have received everything else in my life: the exact same way. My invention, the Schalero® featured on QVC, it was exactly the same. My TEDx talk, it was exactly the same. My doctorate, it was exactly the same. I received healing, deliverances, and soul peace. I could go on for days.

> Providence goes to work when you make a decision.

Creating something from nothing

So, you might say, "Why are my thoughts so important if my heart does the believing?" It's because thoughts are the highway and carrier components of the immaterial to the material. However, it's just as real in the immaterial form as it is in the material form. Well, "What makes it real?" you might ask. Your belief makes it real. "Faith is the substance of things hoped for and the evidence of things not seen" (see Hebrews 11:1). Faith is what hope is made up of. Faith framed GOD's world by HIS Word, so that things which are seen were made not of things that were visible. Life is in out, not out in. We frame our world. Our world doesn't frame us. We have the power to create. God gave us that ability, not the other way around.

> The Word works when you work it.

Just like GOD, who called things which are not as though they were. Scripture after scripture speaks to us about our thoughts and what's in a man.

You have to see what you don't see to see it. Jesus said, "Blessed are those who believe and don't see" (see John 20:29). He was talking about seeing with the physical eyes verses the spiritual eyes. In order to see what you want to see in your life, it first begins with a thought. What you don't see in your life starts by you seeing in your thoughts first. For the things that we see are temporary, the things unseen are eternal (see 2 Corinthians 4:18). 2 Corinthians 5:7 says, "We walk by faith and not by sight." This paradigm shift is the major force of the Christian walk. By focusing our mind's attention on the eternal things of God, we have the proper perspective. We are ready at a moment's notice to walk in our Kingdom dominion, exercising our Kingdom authority, and it starts with how we think. Let's navigate toward the working of miracles the same way we create the life of our dreams with families, houses, and cars.

A Kingdom Mindset - The Ultimate

Jesus' teachings were to shift our mindset to that of Kingdom thinking. That is how blind eyes came open, the lame walked, the dead were raised, withered hands grew, and storms ceased. He came to shift us from fear-based thinking to faith-based thinking. Faith works by love (see Galatians 5:6). We live in a kingdom of love, grace, power, dominion, and authority. This is how it was in the beginning— God's original intent in the Garden of Eden. He has been co-laboring with mankind to bring us back ever since the fall (see 1 Corinthians 3:9).

The Bible says in, 1 Corinthians 2:16, "We have the mind of Christ." We have the capacity as human beings to think like Jesus. Philippians 2:5 says, "Let this mind be in you which was also in Christ Jesus." As human beings we have the power to have the same mind that the resurrected Christ did with all power. Romans 8:27 tells us that the Spirit has a mind. So, by thinking Christ-thoughts we come into perfect alignment with the Spirit of God and our original creative nature, minus all the thoughts from this current evil world.

Philipians 4:8 instructs us to be very intentional about what we think. The tenor of each of our thoughts should be that which is true, noble, just, pure, lovely, of good report, virtuous, and praiseworthy.

Kingdom Thinking = Kingdom Living

This becomes the backdrop and background for everyday miracles. There was not one day when Jesus was not prepared to operate in His Kingdom authority and the Kingdom met the demand. Jesus modeled the same set of actions here on Earth when He performed miracles. The WORD thought thoughts, and He spoke. "Man does not live by bread only but by every Word which proceeds from the mouth of the LORD" (see Deuteronomy 8:3). Jesus said, "My Word is Spirit and Life" (see John 6:63). We need God's word for our spirit to survive just like we need food to eat for our body to survive. Wild thoughts have to be tamed and controlled with God's Word. They can be controlled, and we do not have to be controlled by them. They can be intentionally used for a definite purpose: to create our life. Thoughts can build you up or they can tear you down. In the morning, it takes a minute to switch from thinking about how things were, to how things shall be.

Every day I wake, I create. Every day I have the responsibility of creating the life that I want. I set a vision and work toward achieving that vision with the plans to see that vision come to pass. I complete tasks that work toward achieving my dreams. I finally get to design the life that I want. I

> The Power of Jesus within us gives us the authority to change things on Earth to look like Heaven.

align my vision with the promises of God. There comes a day when you go from wishing and hoping to planning and preparing! I heard the LORD tell me, "Don't settle. Greater is coming." I knew in my heart exactly what He was referring to, and I encourage you to that end. Don't settle for a humdrum life of mediocrity when you can have greater.

I have to fight off evil and negative thoughts that come against me on a daily, sometimes hourly and minute-by-minute, basis. Being nervous and worried takes away my creative

---

Creation happens in real-time and your new life begins to take shape before your very eyes.

---

energy. When I get settled and calm, I make decisions toward my dream life. Then my thoughts begin to form the unseen promises into action. I get what I call "brief flashes of eternity." Going about my day, I begin to see things in my mind that are congruent with my thoughts of what is to come. This is only by being consistent. Consistently creating every day with my thoughts, words, and actions, based on what I believe from the promises of God for me, will happen. I know what's coming. How do you know? I know because I created it!! The life I want and dream of begins to take shape. I can see bits and pieces of it happening every day before my very eyes. When I begin to say, "God, I feel...." He says, "Stop right there. You are not moved by your feelings. You are moved by what you believe and not by shortsighted, short-term, temporary circumstances." "We look not at the things which are seen. For the things which are seen are temporary. We look at the things which are unseen. For the things which are unseen are eternal" (see 2 Corinthians 4:18).

Stay consistent and stay focused.

Think God-sized thoughts, like Jesus did. It starts with what you want! You can't look at what you have. You try and go to precedent. Have I done this before? Has someone in my family done this before? Who do I know who has done this before? Who has ever done this period? You have to have a desire, a target, and a goal. This is what you put all of your faith and energy into. Dream big!! If you don't, life will happen to you instead of you happening to life. Be strengthened. Be encouraged. Be motivated. CREATE!

CHAPTER QUESTIONS

1. What role does your imagination play in seeing your dream life come to pass?

2. Make a list of your own power thoughts and rehearse them over and over.

3. How important is it for your thoughts to line up with the Kingdom of GOD?

Epilogue

As a Christian and as a scientist, I was able to make the connection between the laws that govern the physical world and the laws which govern the spiritual world. It is my hope and prayer that this book will help others to reconcile their thought life and their spiritual life in Christ—with these together the life of their dreams is possible. Equipped with the knowledge of how our thoughts were intended to be used for our advantage, get ready to be empowered! You are about to see things in your life that you did not think could be possible, become possible. The level of joy and contentment is indescribable. Life is now in "reverse-forward." No longer are you striving after things, they now come to you! For more information about the Thoughts Create Workbook and journal, please visit the interactive website at:

www.thoughtscreate.tv.

NOTES

1. NASA, accessed March 31, 2021, https://www.grc.nasa.gov/www/K-12/airplane/newton3.html

2. Guinness Book of World Records, accessed July 23, 2020, https://www.guinnessworldrecords.com/world-records/first-self-made-millionairess

3. Funk & Wagnalls New Comprehensive International Dictionary of the English Language, Deluxe Edition (1980).

4. The Bodner Group, Div. of Chemistry Education, Purdue University, retrieved August 17, 2020, https://chemed.chem.purdue.edu/genchem/topicreview/bp/ch21/chemical.php

5. The Bodner Group, Div. of Chemistry Education, Purdue University, retrieved August 17, 2020, http://chemed.chem.purdue.edu/genchem/history/lavoisier.html

6. Proctor, Bob. "The Law Of Vibration | Bob Proctor | The Secret Law Of Attraction Coaching," Youtube, December 18, 2015, 2:23, https://www.youtube.com/

watch?v=zJ7tJApsKCo

7. "The Man Who Thinks He Can," Walter D. Wintle, accessed June 12, 2020, https://wordinfo.info/unit/4356

8. "I Bargained with Life for a Penny," Jessie B. Rittenhouse, accessed June 12, 2020, https://www.goodreads.com/quotes/430858-i-bargained-with-life-for-a-penny-and-life-would

Look for other resources from this book series:

Book
ebook
Audio Book
Workbook
Bible Study
Special Edition

www.thoughtscreate.tv

THE PRAYER OF SALVATION

Dear Heavenly Father,

I believe that Jesus died for me.

I believe that Jesus paid for my sins on the cross.

I believe that Jesus rose from the dead.

I ask you to forgive me of my sins. I ask you to wash me clean of all sin.

I put my faith and trust in Jesus as my only hope for living eternally with you in heaven.

I ask Jesus to be my Savior and my LORD. I want to live my life for Christ.

I understand that my salvation is not based on my works, but on the sacrifice of Jesus on the cross.

Thank you for saving me.

Amen!

CPSIA information can be obtained
at www.ICGtesting.com
Printed in the USA
BVHW041324260422
635365BV00018B/1643